MY FIRST BOOK ABOUT
JESUS

By Mary Alice Jones
Illustrated
by Robert Hatch

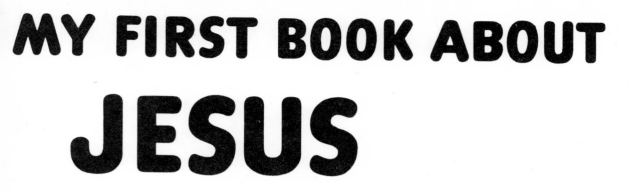

RAND McNALLY & COMPANY

CHICAGO · NEW YORK · SAN FRANCISCO

Designed by Bookservice America, Inc.
Copyright 1953 by Rand McNally & Company
Copyright 1953 under International Copyright Union
by Rand McNally & Company. All rights reserved.
Library of Congress Catalog Card Number: 53-7230
Printed in U.S.A.   Edition of 1958   E

LONG AGO there lived on earth a man
whose name was Jesus.
God sent him to earth to help people.

Jesus was a carpenter.

He made things people needed.

He made them good and strong and sturdy.

Sometimes children played outside the carpenter shop.

Jesus liked to watch them play.

One day Jesus was walking with some friends.
They stopped at a farm.

Jesus said, "The farmer plants the seed.
The seed grows. First a green stem comes up.
It becomes a stalk, heavy with grain.
And all of you are fed.
This is the way God planned it."

One day a sad man came to Jesus.
"My son is very sick," he said.
"Will you help him get well?"
Jesus said, "I will help him. God will show me how.
Your son will get better." And the boy did get well.

Many people came to Jesus.
He needed some helpers.
He asked some fishermen to leave their boats
    and go with him.
The fishermen became Jesus' first helpers.

Jesus liked to have children come to see him.
He told his helpers, "Let the children come to me.
Never tell them I am too busy to see them.
God loves them, every one.
And I love them."

Jesus taught people.

"God wants you to be good to each other," he said.

"If you have two coats and someone else has no coat,
give one of your coats to him.

This is God's plan for you.

This is the way to be happy."

Jesus often told the people stories.
He told a story about a lamb and a shepherd.
A little lamb got lost. Night came.
The little lamb was frightened.

The good shepherd looked and looked
   for the little lamb.
And by-and-by he found it. He took it home again.
The little lamb was glad. The shepherd was glad.

Once Jesus and his friends were in a boat
out on the water.
A storm came up. The friends were afraid.

Jesus said, "Why are you afraid?
God is with you in the storm.
See, the waves are growing still."
So his friends went to work and brought the boat
   to shore.

There was a man who had been unfair.
He had taken more than his share.
Jesus came to see the man. Jesus was friendly.
The man was ashamed of being unfair.
He said, "I will give back all I have taken unfairly."

Often Jesus talked with God.
He loved God. He knew God loved him.
He knew God was helping him every day.
He knew he was God's son.

Jesus taught people about God.
He said, "Look at the bright flowers
and the flying birds.
God takes care of them.

"He loves you much more. Each one of you.
He sends you good gifts of food
    and sunshine and rain.
He helps you when you are lonely or sick or bad."

Once when Jesus was on a trip,
    people had a parade for him.
They brought a donkey for him to ride.
The people marched along waving green branches.

They sang songs of praise.
They wanted to tell Jesus that they loved him.
They wanted to tell God they were glad
Jesus had come.

There were some men who thought God loved them
more than he loved other people.
They turned against Jesus. They hurt him.

But unfriendly men could not get rid of Jesus!
Because what Jesus taught about God was true.
And God was with him.
So Jesus has gone on helping everybody.